H

by Sally Vargas
illustrated by Gabriele Antonini

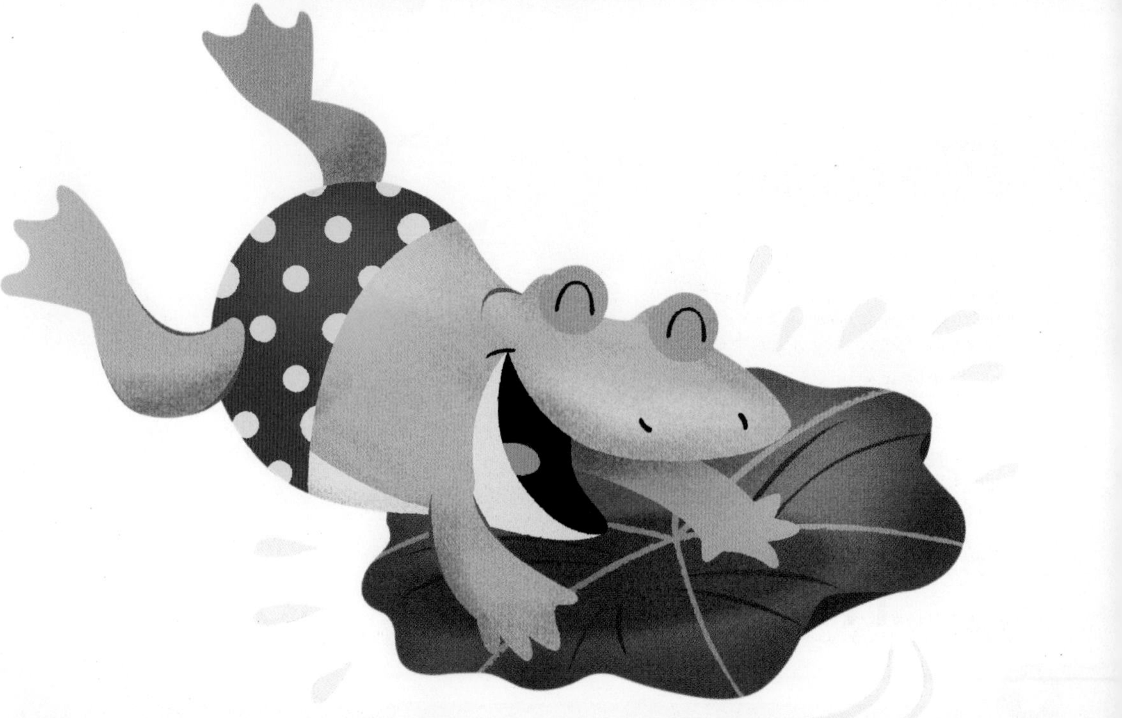

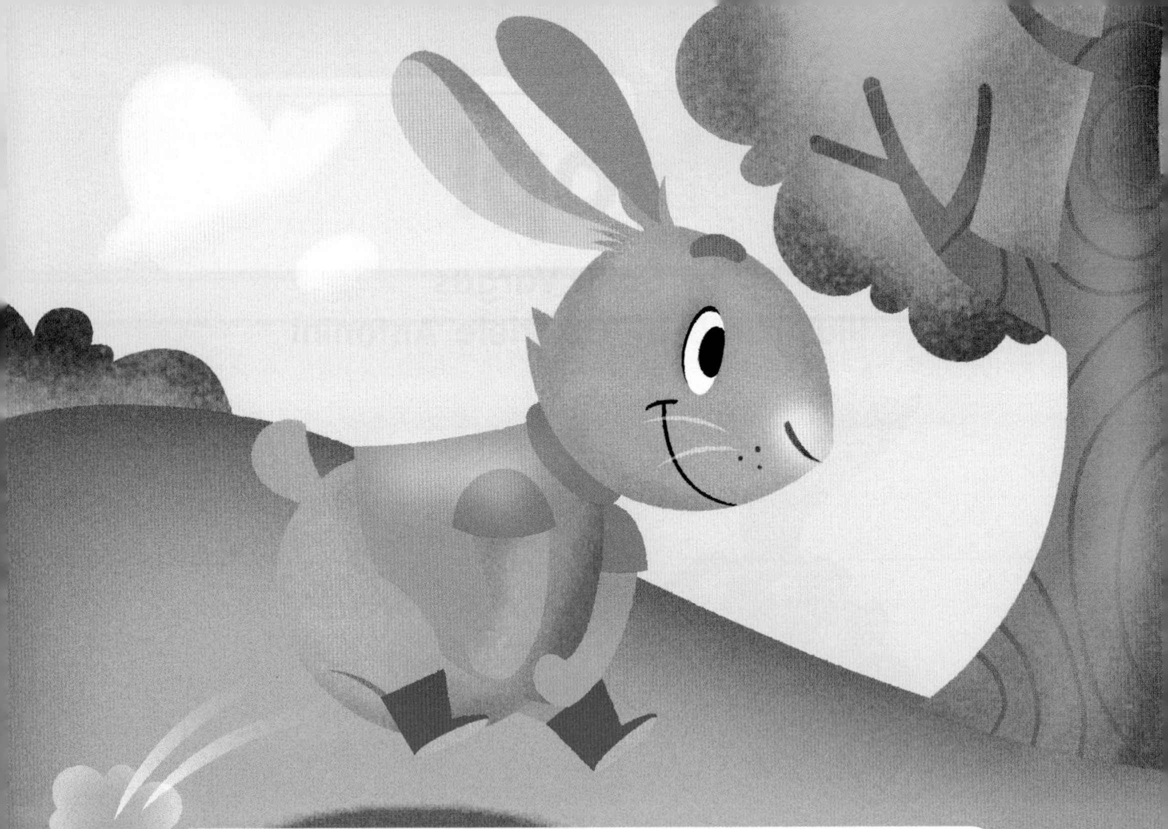

The rabbits can hop.

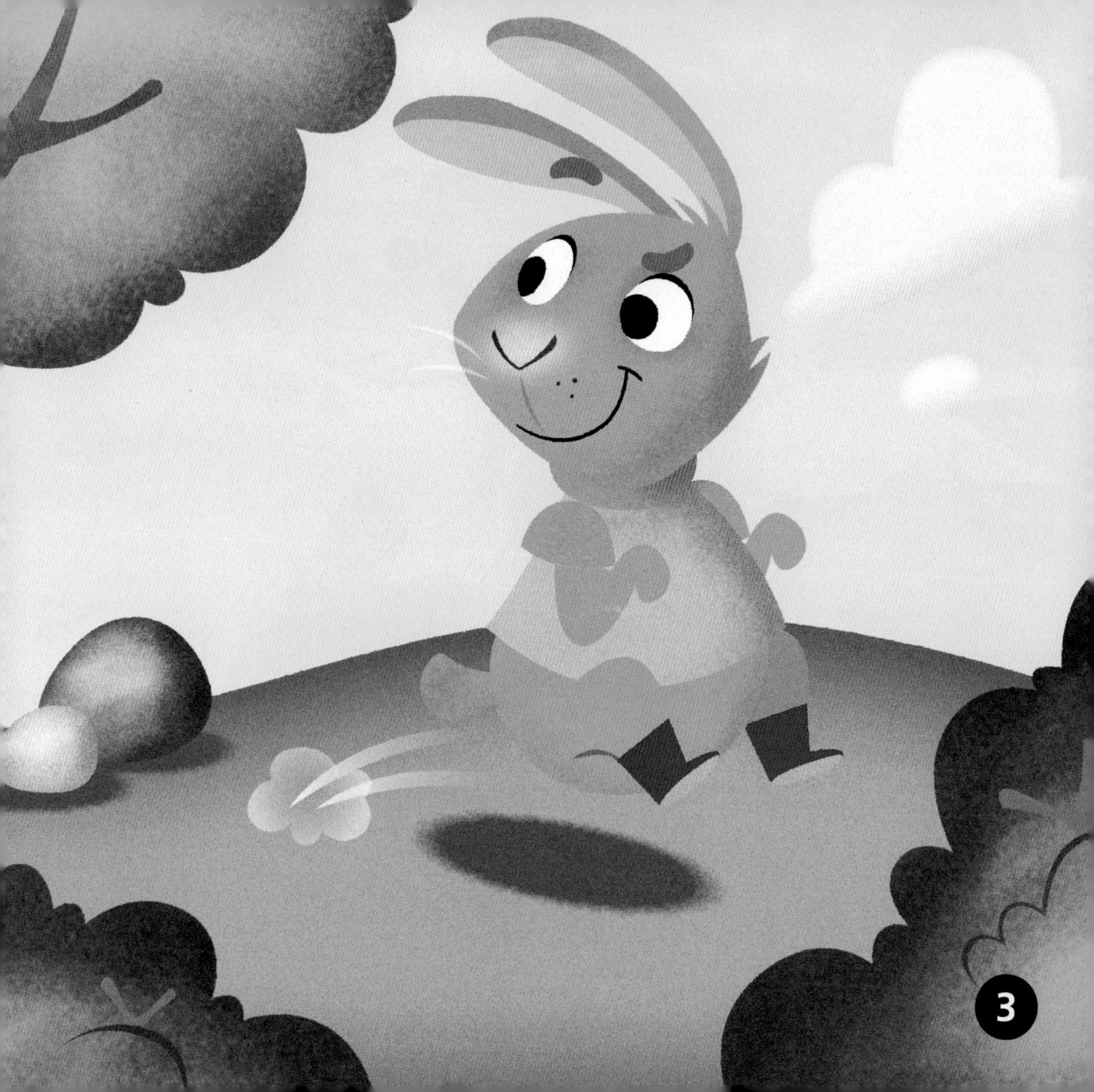

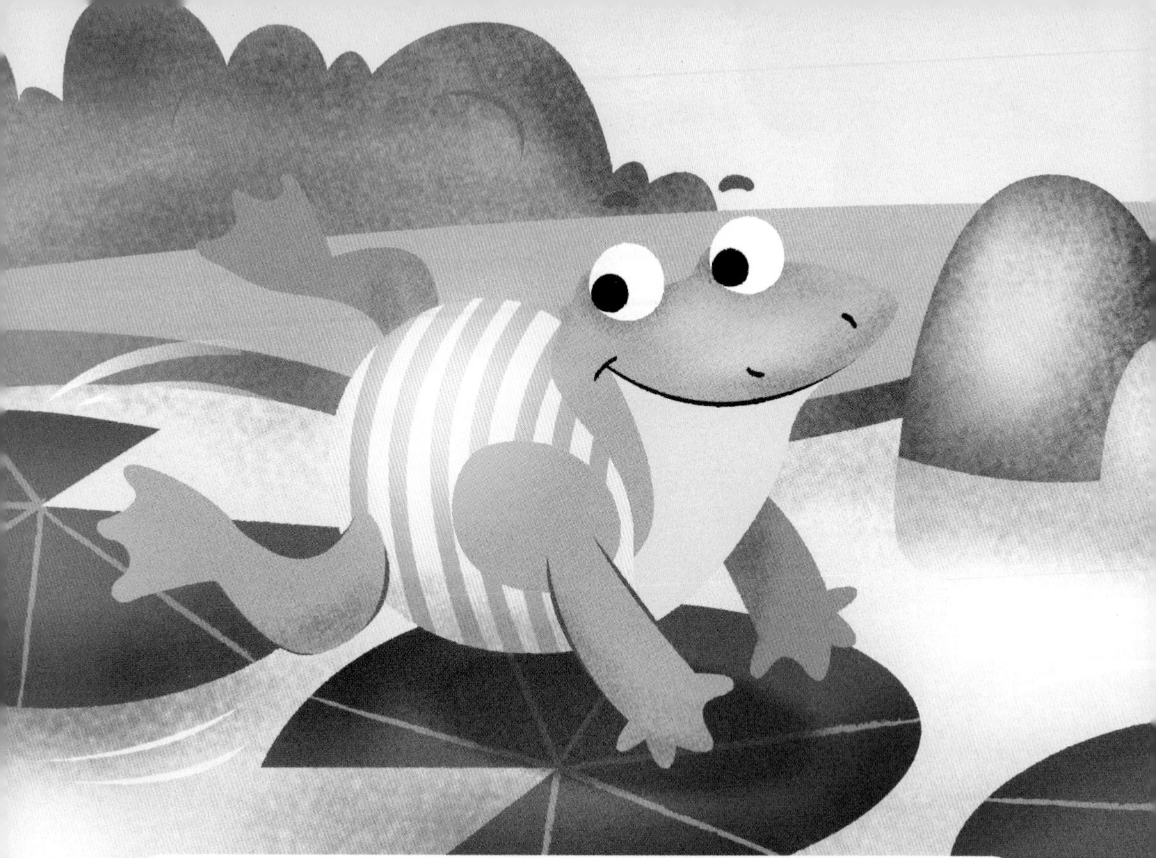

The frogs can hop.

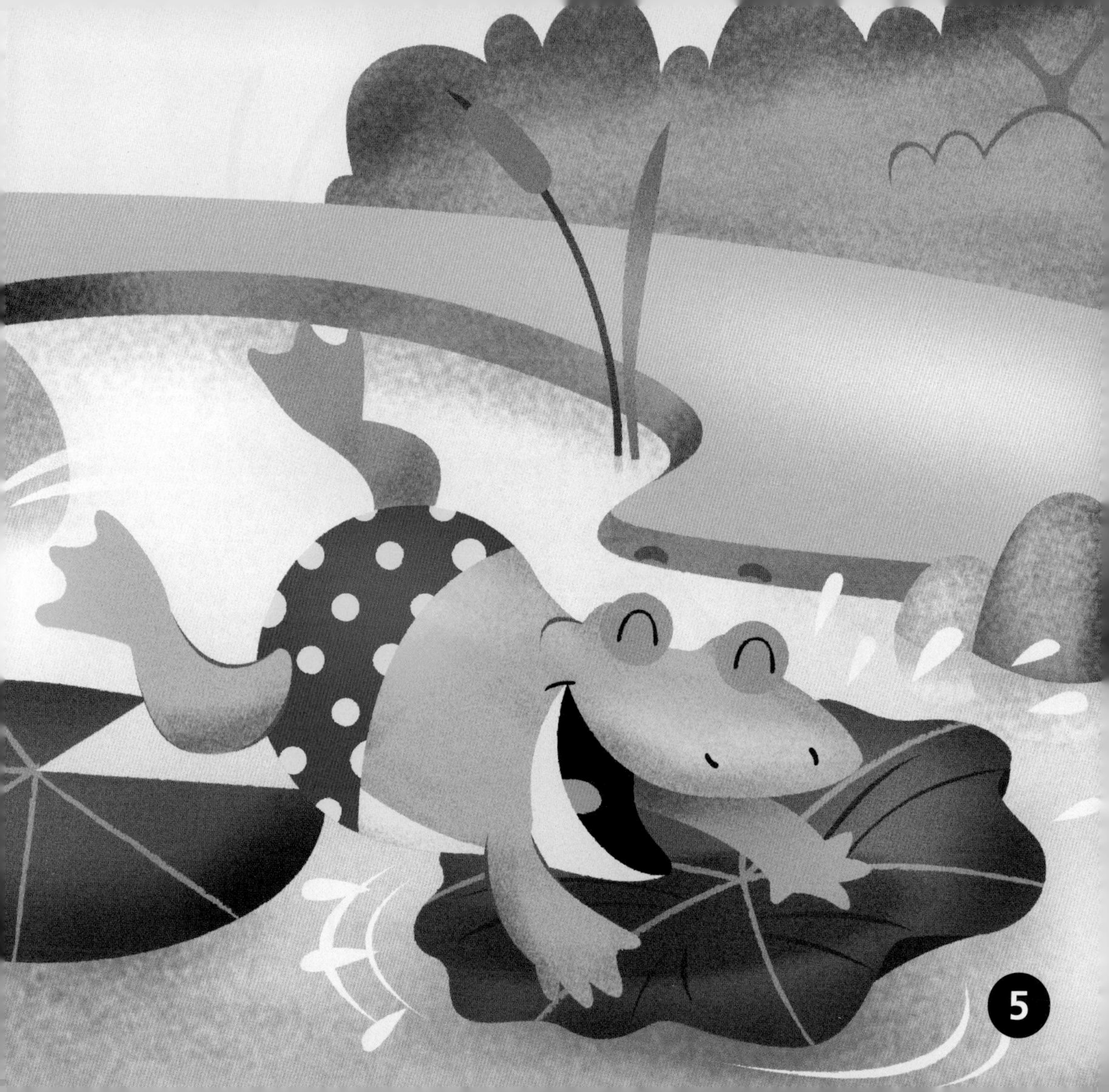

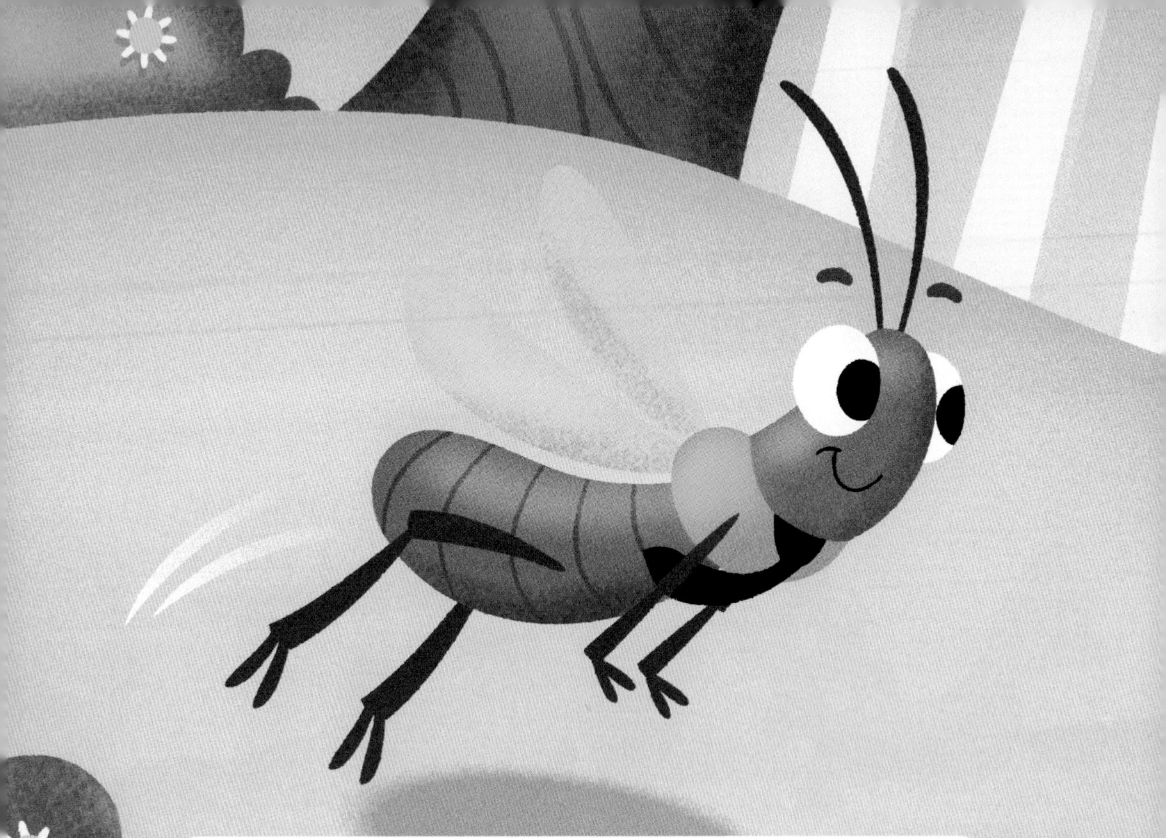

The 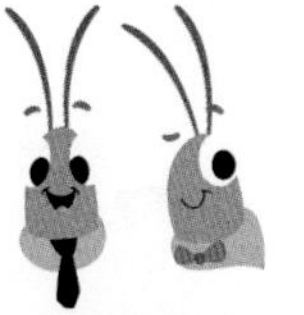 crickets can hop.

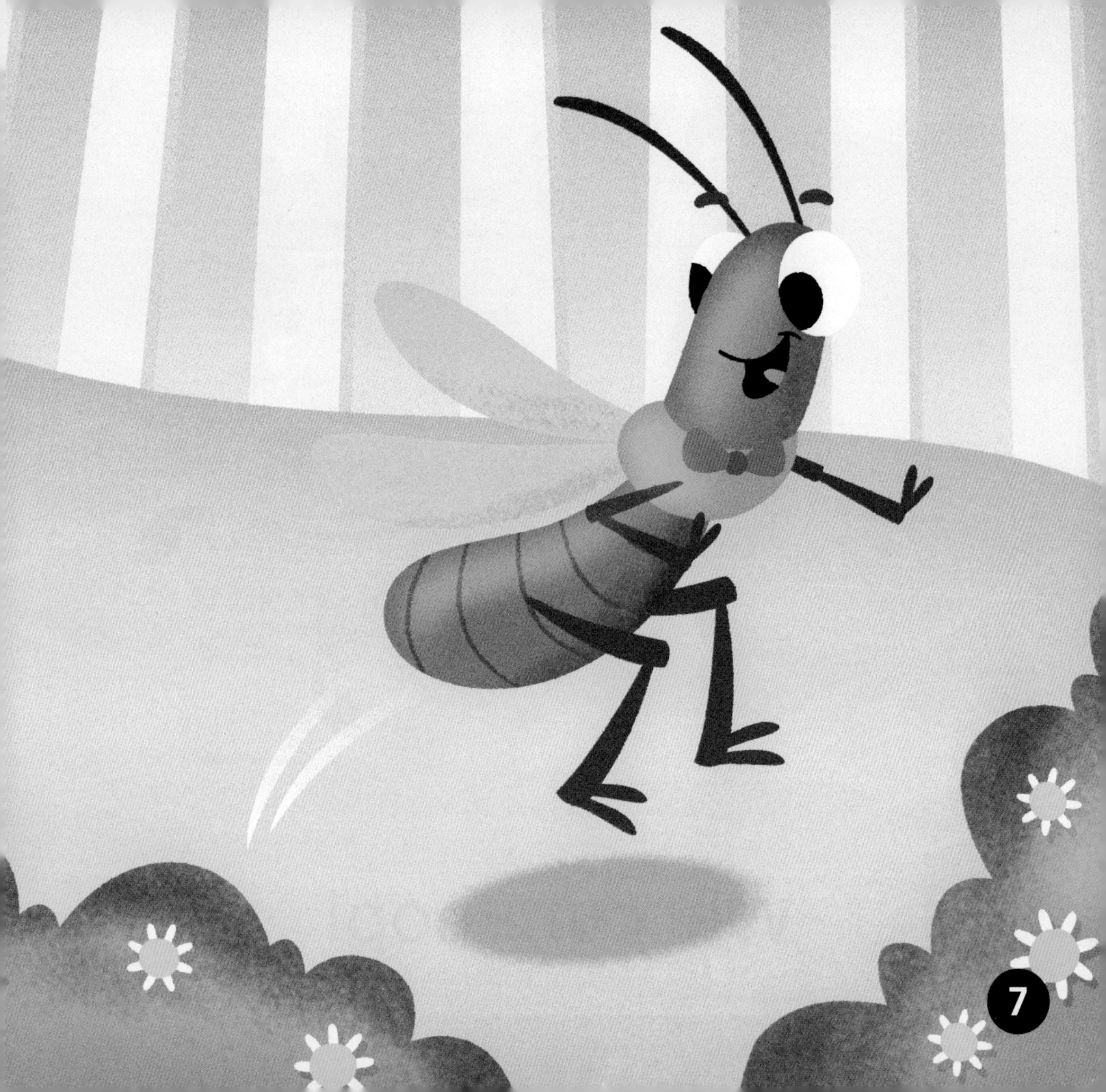

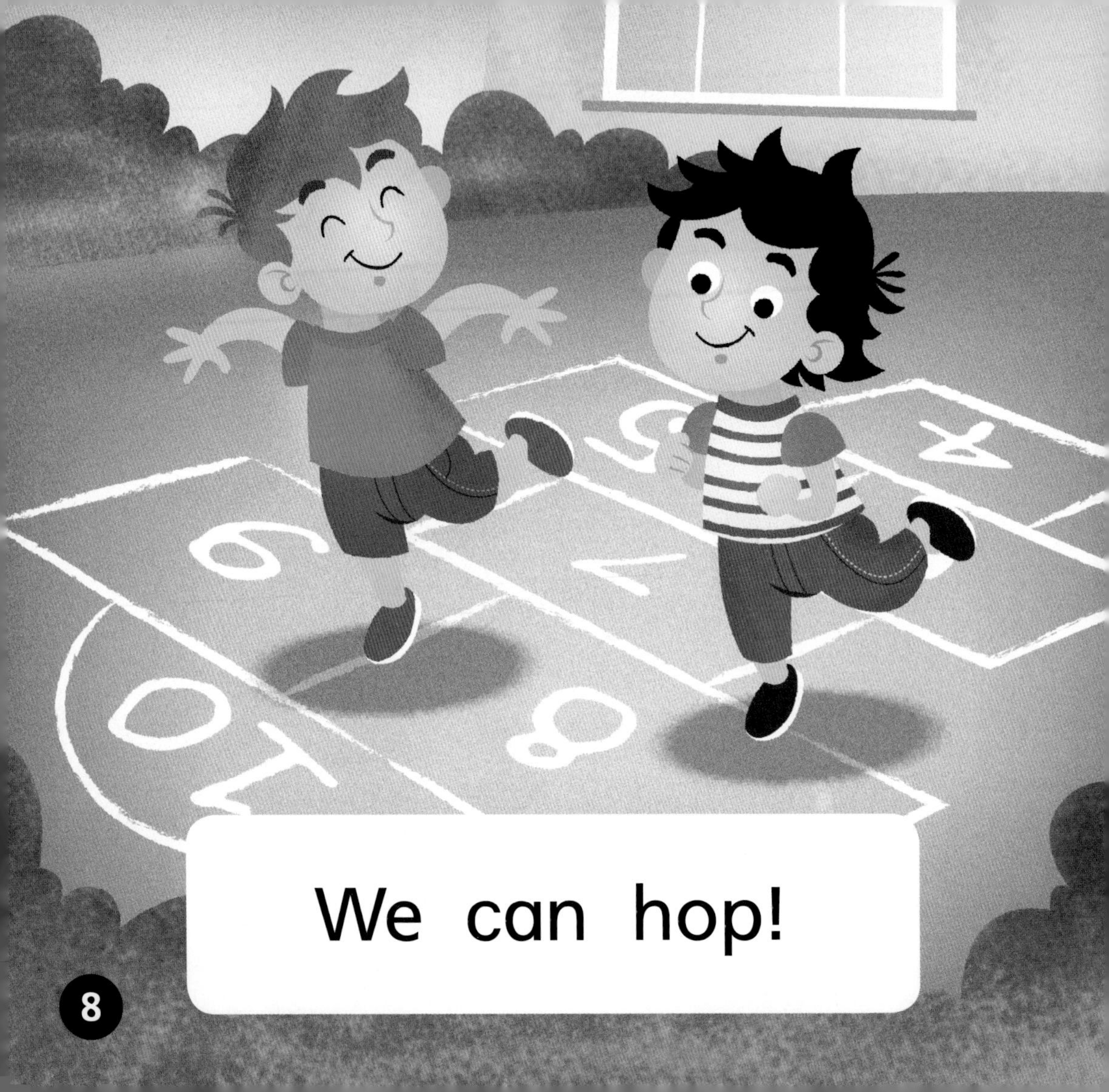

We can hop!